Magic
Johnson

Basketball Immortal

Laurie Rozakis

ROURKE ENTERPRISES,INC.
VERO BEACH, FLORIDA 32964

A Blackbirch Graphics Book.

Library of Congress Cataloging-in-Publication Data

Rozakis, Laurie.
  Magic Johnson / by Laurie Rozakis.
    p. cm. — (The winning spirit)
  Includes index.
  Summary: A biography of the basketball superstar, from his childhood in Michigan through his record-breaking career with the Los Angeles Lakers to his present HIV-positive status.
    ISBN 0-86592-025-7
    1. Johnson, Earvin, 1959–   —Juvenile literature. 2. Basketball players—United States—Biography—Juvenile literature. [Johnson, Earvin, 1959– . 2. Basketball players. 3. Afro-Americans—Biography.] I. Title. II. Series.
GV884.J63R69 1993
796.323'092—dc20
  [B]   92-43275
                                                                         CIP
                                                                          AC

Contents

1

Hoopin' All Day

**"On the court, he's the magic man,
the candy man."**

*T*ime is running short, and the Lakers are only two points ahead of their opponents. Can the team pull off another win? Fans leap from their seats and wave their arms madly. Cheers electrify the arena. Magic Johnson concentrates. He hears only the woosh of sneakers skidding on the floor, the thuds of players bumping into one another, and the coaches screaming from the sidelines.

Suddenly, Magic cuts across the lane, and Kareem flicks him the ball. Magic rotates like lightning and dribbles. Rat-tat-tat-tat-tat-tat-tat-tat! The sound slices through the thick air. His defender freezes for a split second. That's all Magic needs. The ball arcs through the air like a beam of light. Swish! It slips through the net. Magic has done it again!

Opposite: Magic Johnson is undoubtedly one of the greatest athletes of all time. In 1992, he led the U.S. "Dream Team" to a gold medal in the Barcelona Olympics.

In 1980, Earvin "Magic" Johnson became the first rookie in the National Basketball Association (NBA) to be voted Most Valuable Player in the championship finals. A year later, he signed the highest-paying and longest-running contract in the history of basketball. By age 22, he was already a basketball legend. Who is Earvin Johnson?

"On the court, he's the magic man, the candy man," Lakers coach Paul Westhead once remarked. "He throws the ball behind his back, waves to the girls, has fun. But he's also a thug, banging into the boards, knocking people over. Maybe that's why he's magic. Because now you see him, now you don't."

"June Bug"

Earvin Johnson, Jr., was born in the capital city of Lansing, Michigan, on August 14, 1959. He was the fourth of seven children in a working-class family. Chubby before he was tall, people nicknamed him "June Bug."

Lansing was a friendly city made up of many religious and hardworking African-American people. Parents often worked in the automobile and construction industries to make enough money to cover home mortgage and car payments and feed their children. There was rarely money left over for extras. Bicycles, for example, were rare. One year, Magic's father, Earvin, Sr., got together enough money

One of Magic's favorite childhood possessions was a reversible suit jacket. He proudly wore it to church every Sunday.

to buy his son a bike. The child hardly used it, though. No one else on the block owned a bike. There was no one for him to ride with.

The fanciest thing Magic owned was a suit with a jacket that could be worn inside out. Naturally, he wore it only to church. One week, he would wear the black side out; the next week he would turn it to the checkered side. Magic was very proud of that jacket.

A Life of Hard Work

The large Johnson family squeezed into a little yellow house on Middle Street. The house had three bedrooms. Magic's parents had the big bedroom. The three boys—Quincy, Larry, and Magic—shared a room. The four girls—Lily Pearl, Kim, and the twins Evelyn and Yvonne— shared the third bedroom. Until his parents could afford bunk beds, Magic slept in the same bed with Larry. Sometimes, Michael, the first of Mr. Johnson's three children by a previous marriage, lived with the family, too.

To support his large family, Magic's father worked two full-time shifts at General Motors (GM). The first shift began at 5 P.M. The job was a dangerous one. Mr. Johnson worked on the assembly line grinding rough spots from Oldsmobile parts. Sometimes he would come home with his shirt burned to shreds and his skin all red. "I'd like to say it was like death," Mr. Johnson once told his son, "but I've never seen death, so maybe it's worse." Later, he took a less dangerous job with GM. He kept the job for more than 20 years.

Hauling Trash

When Magic was still quite young, his father borrowed some money to buy a second-hand truck. For 19 years, he used the truck to haul trash in between his two shifts at GM. Long before Magic would carry the Lakers to five world championships, he would wake up every Saturday at 7 A.M. to help his father haul trash. Until practice started at 10 A.M., they would collect rubbish, old barrels, bundles of twigs, and bags of garbage. Even that wasn't enough to feed all the Johnson children.

Magic remembers that, "In any garages that used oil, we'd come in while the shop was closed, soap down the floor, let it dry, then come back later and wash it down. Some-times, Dad would go in and scrub the concrete floors after his shift at 2 A.M., then come home and get a few hours sleep, wake up and finish the hauling jobs, take an afternoon nap, then go to work at the plant while the rest of us were sitting down to dinner."

As a kid, Magic spent his Saturday mornings helping his father haul trash around Lansing, Michigan.

Despite this tiring schedule, Mr. Johnson found time to be with his son. On Sunday afternoons the two would sit together on the living room couch and watch NBA games on television. Mr. Johnson, a fine athlete himself, pointed out different strategies to his son. When the game was finished, Magic and his father would go over to the Main Street courts where they would practice the moves they had just seen on television.

Despite his busy work schedule, Magic's father always had time to practice basketball with his talented son.

To whom does Magic credit his success? His father. "He taught me about hard work," Magic says. "He taught me that I wasn't going to get anything in basketball or life without working for it."

When the twins were old enough, Magic's mother, Christine, became a school custodian. Magic remembers how tired she was from working so hard at school and at home. One day Magic saw his mother sitting at the table half-asleep. "Someday I'm going to become somebody, and you won't ever have to work again," he promised her. Magic made good his promise. With his first basketball check, he bought his parents a new house.

Crazy About Basketball

Magic was playing basketball almost from the time he could walk. "I can remember waking up when it was still dark outside," he recalls. "I wanted to play ball so badly that I'd just lie there, looking out the window, waiting for daybreak. If it was too early to go to the schoolyard, I'd dribble on the street. I'd run around the parked cars and pretend they were players on the other team. All up and down Middle Street people used to open their windows and yell at me for waking them up. But I couldn't help it. The game was just in me."

When the neighbors weren't yelling at Magic, they were joking about his devotion to the game. "There goes that crazy June Bug, hoopin' all day," they'd say. On rainy days, he played inside. He'd draw a square on the wall for the hoop and gather up some socks into a ball. The hoop would erase pretty easily, and somehow the socks always seemed to get lost.

"Junior," his mother would yell in the morning, "where did you put all the socks?"

Weeks later, the socks would turn up under the sofa or in the chair cushions. Magic's mom didn't get angry, though. She knew her son was just crazy about basketball.

By fourth grade, Magic was playing on four basketball leagues—at the YMCA (Young Men's Christian Association), the church, the local recreation center, and in the neighborhood. Most often Magic played with his older brother, Larry. But when Larry was too busy, Magic practiced with whomever he could find.

He later said that he spent so much time on the courts that he could have had his mail delivered there. He never imagined that one day children would write letters to him and address them to the Lakers' basketball court!

The Gentle Giant

Magic was six feet tall when he started Dwight Rich Junior High. The seventh grader with the bright smile towered over his classmates. By his second year he was six feet four inches tall. A year later, he was six feet five.

It was in junior high that his name first
appeared in the newspaper. "Earvin Johnson
scored 26 points to lead Rich Junior High to
victory," the article said. "Man, oh man,"
Magic yelled. "Look it here. I didn't know
they were going to do this." He ran to show his
mother. Smiling, she said, "That's nice, Junior."

Magic's reputation spread fast. Athletes
from all over Lansing wanted to play with the
rising star. Magic was so popular that strangers
often stopped him on the street to tell him how
great he was.

Young Magic was very flattered by all the
attention, but he never imagined that he could
actually be a professional basketball player.
His mother wanted him to be a minister. He
always thought he'd be a singer. Magic had
yet to realize the extent of his athletic talent.
Once he did, however, there would be no
turning back.

2

Magic Becomes A Superstar

"That kid has got to be one of the greatest basketball players you'll ever see."

*I*t wasn't until he was in the eighth grade that Magic began to realize he might be a fine basketball player. He thought if he kept getting better, he might be able to play on the Sexton High School team, and that would really be something. He never imagined a college basketball career—and certainly never the National Basketball Association.

Sexton High School was well known across Michigan for its great basketball team. The school had only black students. Since it was just five blocks from his home, Magic never dreamed that he would end up going anywhere else. But he hadn't counted on busing.

14

"Busing" was established to make sure each school had a balanced number of black and white students. Some students from mainly black neighborhoods traveled by bus to schools with mostly white students. And some in white neighborhoods went to school in black neighborhoods. Magic's family lived just outside the cutoff line. Suddenly, he could no longer go to Sexton High. Instead, he had to take a bus to Everett High School. This was an all-white school on the south side of Lansing. It was about 15 miles from his house. Magic was very angry. He even wrote a letter of complaint to the school board.

At first, things did not go well at Everett. Magic and his fellow black classmates were only the second group of black students to attend the high school. The one hundred black students from Sexton always sat together at basketball games. It was a long time before he felt comfortable in his new surroundings.

Looking back, Magic now sees that busing was one of the best things that happened to him. He had not known many white people. Being at Everett High School showed him a whole new side to life, and it taught him how to deal with white people.

Magic Meets Dr. Charles Tucker

Magic's life improved even more when he met Dr. Charles Tucker, the school system's

Magic's early mentor was Dr. Charles Tucker, a young school psychologist who had once played professional basketball.

psychologist. Magic immediately took to the 27-year-old black man after Dr. Tucker beat the pants off him during a one-on-one game. Dr. Tucker had not stopped to tell Magic that he had played pro basketball!

Soon, Dr. Tucker was acting like a second father to Magic. The two often played a lot of ball together on local courts. Dr. Tucker taught Magic all the tricks of professional basketball. He showed Magic how to play defense and offense. Dr. Tucker even took Magic to Detroit, Chicago, and Indianapolis to watch professional players. Magic almost flipped when

Dr. Tucker personally introduced him to Kareem Abdul-Jabbar, one of the greatest basketball players of all time. Dr. Tucker and Magic talked about it all the way home.

"You just take care of yourself," Dr. Tucker said. "Work real hard, and don't let anything come between you and winning, and someday some kid will shake your hand and brag to his partners about it." Time would prove Dr. Tucker right on many occasions!

"Magic" Is Born

Magic continued to blossom on the court, and, soon his career reached a turning point. Everett High School was slated to play Jackson Parkside School. The Jackson Parkside team was heavily favored to win because of its good players. But the Everett team swept to victory. The opposing coach said to Magic's coach, "That kid has got to be one of the greatest basketball players you'll ever see." Magic remembers it as the best game of his entire life. Magic scored 36 points, pulled down 18 rebounds, and made 16 assists.

After the game, reporters crowded around Magic. Everyone was shouting questions at him. Fred Stabley, Jr., a sportswriter for the *Lansing State Journal*, went into the locker room as he always did. This time, though, he waited until everyone had left. Then he went over to Magic.

"Earvin, that was some performance out there tonight," he said. "I think you should have a nickname. I was thinking of calling you Dr. J., but that's taken. So is Big E—Elvin Hayes." He paused for a moment. "How about if I call you Magic?" he asked.

Earvin thought for a second. "Magic," he said. "Okay. Sounds good to me!"

The Recruiters

Magic led his team to the Class A quarterfinals when he was a sophomore, to the semifinals when he was a junior, and to the championship when he was a senior. He drew people to Everett's basketball games like—well, magic. Businesspeople wanted Magic to appear at their stores. Fans tried to get tickets to games. And college recruiters flocked to get a glimpse of the young athlete's amazing skill.

Magic was only 15 when the first college offered him a basketball scholarship. Within months, the invitations were pouring in. For the next two years, the school received more mail addressed to Magic than to everyone else in the school combined. Every school in the country that had a basketball team wanted Magic for their team.

The principal's secretary sent polite letters refusing the offers. That didn't stop some of the recruiters. They telephoned Magic's house day and night. They grabbed him in school. They even showed up on his doorstep. Some tried to influence his mother. Others offered him money and fancy cars. Magic refused these people right away. He even refused to accept free meals. When he went to lunch and dinner with recruiters, Dr. Tucker paid the bill so Magic did not have to accept anything.

Magic narrowed his choice down to a few schools: Michigan State, the University of Michigan, Notre Dame, Maryland, and North Carolina. He asked his parents and Dr. Tucker for help in picking the school. "The choice is yours," they would always answer. Secretly, though, his parents wanted him to go to the University of Michigan or Michigan State so that he could be closer to home. They liked having him and his sunny smile around.

Choosing a College

By his senior year, Magic had narrowed his choices down to the University of Michigan and Michigan State. Dr. Tucker and Magic's father favored Michigan State because it was in Lansing. That way, they could go to every one of Magic's games. But Magic's mother voted for the University of Michigan. She was more concerned with Magic's education than with basketball. The University of Michigan had a better reputation for studies than Michigan State. She believed that education was the key to any success. "What will you do when you are too old to play ball?" she asked Magic. "The more education you have, the more doors will open for you," she argued.

The deadline was coming up fast. Magic could wait no longer. Which school would it be, the University of Michigan or Michigan State?

The press conference was mobbed. People came from all over the country to hear Magic's decision. There were scouts and fans from as far away as Chicago, New York, Florida, and Washington, D.C. What would Magic say? He announced, "Michigan State!" The audience went wild.

"Why would you pick Michigan State when you could go anywhere in the country?" they all asked.

"I grew up here and always dreamed that someday I would wear the green and white," Magic answered with a big smile. "When it came right down to it, I don't think I could have gone anywhere else."

The crowd of sportswriters and local radio reporters persisted "But why Michigan State over the University of Michigan?" they asked. "The University's team, the Wolverines, are on national television. They are famous."

"I like the underdog school," Magic tried to explain. "Every team I've played on was not supposed to win. But they all did. Why? Because they work hard as a team."

3

The Magic Touch

**"Winning means playing
an inner game within
yourself, not against
someone else."**

Michigan State's basketball team
needed some magic. The team had suffered
a great deal of trouble in the past few years.
Players were squabbling with one another.
Some had even been suspended from the team
for fighting. The coach had been replaced.
The last time the team had won a championship was 17 long years ago—in 1959. The past
year had been dismal. The team went 10–17.
People all over campus stopped Magic to say,
"Thanks for choosing us. We need you!"

They also showed their support at the ticket
booth. For the first time in the history of the
college, all 9,886 seats in the Jenison Field
House were snapped up when there was a
basketball game being played. People fought

so fiercely for tickets that the athletic office had to use a lottery system.

The First Game

The season opened against Central Michigan. The game had been sold out since April, when Magic signed his letter of intent to go to Michigan State. Was he nervous the night before his first college game? You bet! He tossed and turned all night long. Great plays from the past raced through his mind like a speeded-up movie. The sound of a great dunk echoed over and over. The crowd roared in his ears. So many people were counting on him. Could he do it again tomorrow?

By morning, the butterflies in his stomach were the size of bats. His heart thumped against his ribs. He was sweating. Taking a deep breath, Magic made his way into the arena. The cheering shook the stadium from top to bottom. Even the windows rattled.

Magic wasn't the only player with bat-sized butterflies. Everyone felt the pressure. With a leap, they jumped into action. The battle was a tough one, but the team fought together and victory was theirs! Magic scored seven points, nine rebounds, and eight assists. Not a bad beginning, but he was disappointed. He sat for hours and studied movies of the game. What could he have done better? Would his fans wonder where the Magic had gone?

Magic returned home to Lansing, Michigan, after being named Most Valuable Player in the 1979 NCAA tournament.

Within two weeks the team had become strong and confident. They won four of their five games. The press zoomed in on Magic! He felt upset that his teammates would think he was trying to get all the attention. He spoke to them, but they already knew that Magic was a team player. He saw his job as getting the ball to the team's high scorers: Jay Vincent, Greg Kelser, Don Bergovich, and Terry Donnaly.

The year only got better. The team began its Big Ten meet in January with only one loss. When it was all over, the Michigan Spartans took home their first Big Ten title in 19 years. In Magic's first year, the Spartans won 25 games and suffered only 5 losses.

Falling in Love

Despite his heavy playing schedule, Magic continued to work hard at his schoolwork and earned a B average. He was studying communications so he could be a sportscaster when his playing days were over. In his spare time, he worked as a disc jockey at a local disco. He called himself "E.J. the DeeJay."

He also found time to date. "I do like the ladies," he once told a reporter in a newspaper interview. The lady he liked most was Earleatha "Cookie" Kelly. They spent hours talking about the future. "I knew even then I wanted to marry her," he later said.

Magic wasn't the only basketball player falling in love. During his second year at Michigan State, most of Magic's teammates bought diamond engagement rings for their girlfriends as Christmas gifts. The players didn't have a lot of money, and the diamonds were very small. But Magic couldn't even afford the 50 dollars for one of those rings. Cookie was the only one of the group that didn't receive a diamond ring for Christmas.

"I'm not gonna buy you some cheap ring from a Cracker Jack box," Magic told her. "Someday I'll buy a *real* diamond. And when I do, you'll be able to see that thing all the way from the other side of the court." It took him almost 14 years to do it, but Magic made good on his promise.

Turning Pro?

Halfway through Magic's first year, the Kansas City Kings called his father. They wanted to see if Magic would leave college and become a professional basketball player. Even though Magic was only 18, he could become a pro under the NBA's "hardship" rule. It was easy to do. Magic didn't even have to prove that he needed the money. His parents and Dr. Tucker were very much against the idea, but they left the decision in Magic's hands.

Magic felt good about being asked to join a professional team. It showed that people recognized his talent. Also, he would make a great deal of money as a professional basketball player—$250,000 a year for six years. But there were drawbacks, too. If he turned pro, he could not play in the Olympics. He'd be throwing away the chance to win an NCAA (National Collegiate Athletic Association) championship as well. He'd miss out on all the fun of college life. If he passed up this chance, would he have it again in the future? Could he stay uninjured long enough to become a pro when he finished his college education?

The more he thought about it, though, the more he decided it was not right for him—yet. He wanted to stay in college. His parents and Dr. Tucker were very happy. Magic decided to forget about the offer and turn his mind back to education. The matter was closed—or was it?

Once the press found out about it, they kept after him. "Are you turning pro, Magic?" "When will you make your decision?" "What team will you pick?" Magic had no answers—he had no idea what he wanted to do.

The Second Season

Magic had become the team leader. He shouted directions, praise, and congratulations to the players. "Way to go!" he'd shout. He was also quick to apologize if he hurt another player with a quick pass.

Paired with forward Gregory Kelser in a brutal pass-and-dunk operation, Magic had a thrilling second year. He averaged 17.5 points, 7.3 rebounds, and 8.4 assists a game. His total of 269 assists is a school record that no one has yet broken.

Michigan trounced Indiana, 75–64, to win the NCAA tournament in 1979. Magic was named the championship tournament's most valuable player—beating out Indiana's forward Larry Bird, another superb passer. Thanks to his team's support, Magic scored 24 points, the highest in the game. As a result, he was voted an All-American. The Chicago *Tribune* voted him Most Valuable Player in the Big Ten.

With all Magic's success and talent, people began to wonder if he had outgrown Michigan. Was he thinking of moving on? Was this the time for him to turn pro?

4

Magic Joins the Lakers

"He does so many incredible things on the court that you want to help him keep doing them. It's really good to play with him."

Most Valuable Player, All-American, the NCAA title: Magic had won all the awards. These victories made him worth a great deal of money to professional basketball teams. Magic decided the time was right to leave college and become a professional basketball player. His mother, though, was very much against his decision.

"What will you do if you get injured?" she asked. "Even if you stay healthy, one day you will be too old to play ball. What then? If you stay in college, you can get a good job when your playing days are done." Over and over, she urged her son to stay in college. Magic wasn't sure what to do. He decided to wait to see which team wanted him—and how much money they offered him.

On April 19, 1979, the commissioner of the NBA flipped a coin to decide whether Chicago or Los Angeles would have first choice of the college players. The Los Angeles Lakers won the flip. Magic knew that Chicago really wanted him. Did the Lakers?

Yes! Jack Kent Cooke, the Lakers' owner, called Magic and said, "We have to talk about your future." Magic hired a team of lawyers to help him read through all the contracts and make the right decision. It took some time to work out an agreement. How much money would make Magic decide to leave college?

Bargaining with the Lakers

When Magic was in his first year at Michigan State, Kansas City had offered him $250,000 a year. He knew the Lakers would have to offer him more than that. It couldn't be more than $650,000, though. That was what they were paying Kareem Abdul-Jabbar. It was right for Kareem to get the most money. He was a great player with a lot of experience.

Dr. Tucker thought the Lakers would offer $500,000. Magic, his father, and Dr. Tucker decided that was a good offer. If the Lakers offered Magic $500,000, he would join the team. If the Lakers offered less, he would stay at Michigan State at least another year.

Magic wanted more than just money. He decided that he had to be the first player picked

Magic's decision to join the Lakers in 1979 altered basketball history forever.

in the draft. This would give him even more power. Magic also wanted a guarantee that he would not, under any circumstances, be cut from the team. If he got sick or injured, he would still be entitled to all the money. If any advertising opportunities came up, Magic wanted to be able to take advantage of them. Basically, Magic wanted to make sure both he and his family were well provided for—no matter what.

The Lakers' first offer was $400,000. Magic asked for $600,000. After days of talking, the Lakers offered $500,000. Magic accepted and became the highest-paid rookie in NBA history. Even so, his mother made him promise to finish college. Magic promised.

On May 16, 1979, Magic announced he would sign with the L.A. Lakers as a first-round draft pick. Standing with Magic is Lakers coach Jerry West.

Magic gets hugs from his parents after signing with the L.A. Lakers on June 25, 1979, at the Plaza Hotel in New York City.

The Pressure Mounts

"Ladies and gentlemen, this is one of the most historic events in Laker history," said the press agent welcoming Magic to the Lakers. Little did he know how true his greeting would be.

There was a lot of pressure on Magic to make the Lakers a more exciting team. Fans thought the Lakers were getting boring. Fewer people were coming to the games. Magic had pressure in other ways, too. Los Angeles was very different from Lansing. There were strange faces and unfamiliar places. It took time for

Magic easily won over teammates and fans with his remarkable talent and friendly smile.

Magic to get used to the freeways, dreary weather, and smog. Magic was only 19 years old. Could he come through for the team—and for himself?

Smashing to Victory

Magic was so enthusiastic that his teammates couldn't believe he was for real. Right away, he became friendly with everyone on the team. His smile made everyone smile with him. Magic knew that he had a gift for making teams come together. He knew that people liked him for his hard work and good spirits. He worked his special brand of magic, and the Lakers changed from a group of stiff winners to a good basketball team that played with passion. By the middle of March, the Lakers had taken off like a rocket to Mars! Now, there was no slowing them down.

By smashing Seattle 131–108, the Lakers took the lead in the NBA's Pacific Division. On March 23, they seized first place with a 101–96 victory over Utah. In the play-offs, the Lakers trounced the Phoenix Suns and Seattle Sonics before coming face to face with the Philadelphia 76ers in the finals. Kareem had a bad ankle so he couldn't play. The most important game of the finals belonged to Magic. It was May 16, 1980.

Magic started as center. Then the coach gave him the go-ahead, and Magic was off.

Low- and high-post center positions, point guard, shooting guard, small forward, and power forward—Magic was all over! For 47 minutes, he led his team in scoring. The ball slipped through the hoop 42 times. The crowd went wild. Magic led in rebounds, too, and had seven assists. The Lakers finished with a 123–107 victory. It was their first world title since 1972. Magic had played one of the greatest games in the history of basketball.

When the dust settled, Magic had set an amazing number of records. He made 503 baskets out of the 949 he tried. This gave him a .530 percentage, setting a Lakers' rookie record. That's not all! He set another rookie record with 563 assists. And another with 374 free-throws out of 462.

He was as modest as always. "Kareem brought us here," he said. "Without the Big Fella, we wouldn't be here. We won it for him and for ourselves." But people recognized Magic's amazing power. He was named Most Valuable Player. "He does so many incredible things on the court that you want to help him keep doing them. It's really good to play with him," said one of his teammates.

Sidelined by Injuries

In November of 1980, Magic was still on top of the world. He felt great and it showed in his performance. The Lakers had won 15 of their

20 games. Magic was averaging 21.4 points a game—up 3.4 from his previous year's average. He was leading the NBA in steals and assists. What could go wrong? Plenty!

The next night, the Lakers were playing against the Atlanta Hawks. Magic's knee was raked by another player's heavy knee brace. It felt a little tingly, but Magic kept on playing. On the fifth night, the same knee was again smashed by someone on the other team. He crashed to the floor in terrible pain. The manager immediately wrapped Magic's knee in ice, but it was too late. The damage was done. "You'll need surgery," the doctor told Magic. "You have a torn ligament." After the operation, Magic was in a cast from his waist to his toes. Then came weeks of painful exercise. Magic practiced on the court and in the gym until he was back to his old self, but by that time, he had missed 45 games.

Magic later said that the pain in his leg was nothing compared with the pain in his heart. The entire season was over for him, he thought. And if he didn't heal well, his entire career might be over. The Lakers played well without him, but their "heart" was missing. "When Magic returned it was like Looney Tunes," said the coach. "Everybody started laughing again. It was unreal."

The Lakers decided to take steps to keep Magic in Los Angeles forever. In 1981, they

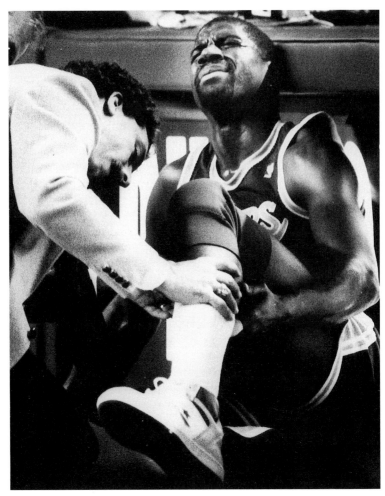

Magic cringes in pain after colliding with another player in a game against the Phoenix Suns in 1987.

added a 25-year extension to Magic's contract. He would be paid a million dollars a year in cash. This made him the highest paid basketball player in the world. The following year, the Lakers swept the conference play-offs. They went on to win the NBA championships.

Magic had the world on a string. But his string would later break with a sudden cruel and vicious snap.

5

AIDS

"What I've learned is that life doesn't stop....You've got to keep...fighting and living life with the same attitude as before."

*W*hen he wasn't on center court, Magic was enjoying his new life. He bought a gold Mercedes (an expensive German automobile) and started exploring Los Angeles nightlife. He and his friends boogied far into the night at all the "in" spots in town. Magic carried his high spirits wherever he went—even into the air! Sometimes when the team was flying to a game, Magic would break loose and dance in the aisles with the flight attendants. "Old E.J. the DeeJay was born to make people have a good time," he would often say. Women mobbed him. But Magic never forgot his first love, Cookie Kelly. On September 14, 1991, Cookie and Magic were married in Lansing,

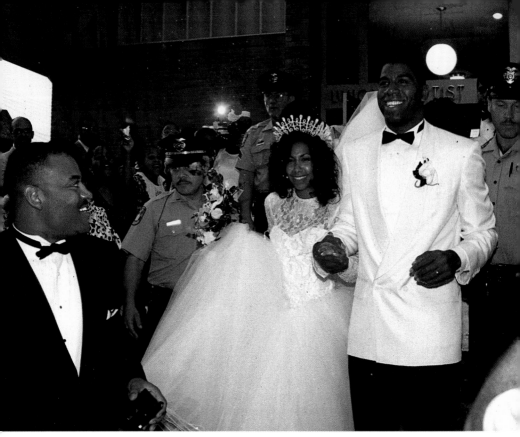

Magic never forgot his first love, Cookie Kelly. The couple married on September 14, 1991.

Michigan. Magic said that it was the happiest day of his life. But just a few weeks later, his world came crashing down.

Tragedy Strikes

On October 25, 1991, Magic went to find out why he had been refused a life-insurance policy. "Earvin, sit down," the doctor said. "You have the HIV virus."

AIDS (Acquired Immune Deficiency Syndrome) develops as a result of the HIV virus. The disease destroys a person's ability to fight illnesses. AIDS itself doesn't kill people. It weakens their bodies so they die of another disease. Magic had gotten the HIV virus from having unprotected sex. He admitted this publicly because he wanted to prevent others from making the same mistake.

People everywhere were shocked by the news about Magic. They fear he will develop AIDS before a cure can be found. Magic was strong and courageous. He smiled and told people they did not have to be afraid. Magic promised to do everything he could to stay healthy for a long time. He now takes medicine to try to hold off the disease.

On November 7, 1991, Magic announced that because he had tested positive for the HIV virus he was retiring from basketball.

Magic thought long and hard about what the doctor had said. He wanted to find a way to make some good come out of his illness. He decided to help spread the word about AIDS. Maybe he could help some people by showing that he would not give up, he thought. The world responded. More than 200,000 letters arrived within two weeks. Magic continues to get thousands of letters each week. He has been overwhelmed with support. To back up his words of advice, Magic served for awhile on the President's National Commission on AIDS. He works to educate others, especially young people, about AIDS prevention and awareness. He teaches people simple ways to protect themselves from AIDS.

In 1992, Magic criticized President Bush for not doing enough to end the AIDS crisis.

Leaving the Lakers

Magic felt as good as ever but wondered if he could give the Lakers one hundred percent. After much careful thought, he finally reached a decision. On November 7, 1991, Magic announced his retirement from basketball. "I'm going to miss playing," he said. "But I'm going to deal with it and my life will go on." He had played for 12 years.

Magic's Back

Magic, however, couldn't stay down for long. On February 9, 1992, he traveled to Orlando, Florida, to play in the All-Star Game. His teammates backed up his decision to return to the game. The fans showed their support, too. The crowd started screaming even before Magic walked in. "Don't cry," he told himself. "Stay strong for all the people."

After the game, all his old friends gathered in the locker room to show him their support. Many of his fellow basketball players were there. Friends from Lansing had flown in. His relatives were crowded around. His fifth-grade coach, Jim Dart, was about to cry. "You know," he said, "every warrior dies on the battlefield. Every great general goes down in the end. This is where you belong. If you're going to die, let it be on the court, doing what you love to do, what you were born to do." Magic took Jim's advice.

During the summer of 1992, Magic joined the best basketball players in the country to play on the Olympic "Dream Team" in Barcelona, Spain. His teammates said to him, "You look too good. You're coming back, man." He led the team to a gold medal. "He's a class act and a tremendous player," his teammates said. He called the awards ceremony "the greatest moment of my life."

"What I've learned is that life doesn't stop. You don't die. You've got to keep going, keep on working, fighting and living life with the same attitude as before," he said soon after.

On January 11, 1992, Magic received the NAACP Image Award for his work in the fight against AIDS. Standing with Magic is talk-show host Arsenio Hall.

Magic Johnson and Michael Jordan, members of the 1992 U.S. Olympic basketball team, hold up their new uniforms during a charity benefit for the Michael Jordan Foundation in 1991.

On September 29, 1992, Magic announced that he would be playing for the Lakers again on a limited 50 to 60 game schedule. This meant that he would be missing only about 20 games during the season. What made him decide to play again? It wasn't the money. He has millions of dollars. According to his wife, "Earvin is coming back simply because he loves the game, and feels as if it had been

Magic called winning the gold medal in Barcelona, "the greatest
moment of my life."

snatched away from him. He didn't want some
doctors telling him he couldn't play anymore."

"Things are coming up all the time," he
said in a recent interview in *People Weekly*
magazine. "If you take care of yourself and
your attitude is right and you just take it day
to day, then things will work out."

"I'm Gone for Good"

Controversy swirled around Magic's medical
condition. Could the HIV virus be transmitted
during a game? "I don't think his playing basketball is a life-threatening situation—either for
him or anybody else," said Dr. Alan Ginsberg,
a researcher at Johns Hopkins University. But
during the Lakers' final pre-season game, Magic
got scratched on his arm. It wasn't bleeding
much, and he put a bandage and a sweatband
over it, but concern still mounted.

On November 7, 1992, Magic chose to
retire for a second time. "This time," he said,
"it's for good." All the publicity about his
medical condition had affected the Lakers.
"Various controversies surrounding my return
are taking away from both basketball and the
larger issue of living with HIV," he said. "I've
come to realize that it simply isn't possible to
return to playing in the NBA and still continue
to be involved in all the things I want to do."
As always, Magic made his decision first and
foremost to help his team.

Glossary

AIDS Acquired Immune Deficiency Syndrome caused by the HIV virus.

busing Mixing races by mixing schools.

HIV The virus that attacks the immune system and causes AIDS.

ligament A large muscle.

rebound To capture a basketball as it comes off the backboard.

rookie First-year player.

virus Organism that invades cells in the body.

For Further Reading

Greenberg, Keith. *Magic Johnson: Backcourt Wizard*. Minneapolis, MN: Lerner, 1972.

Gutman, Bill. *Magic Johnson: Hero on and off Court*. Brookfield, CT: Millbrook, 1992.

Johnson, Rick. *Magic Johnson: Basketball's Smiling Superstar*. New York: Dillon, 1992.

Levin, Rich. *Magic Johnson: Court Magician*. Chicago: Childrens Press, 1981.

Index

Photo Credits:
Cover: Wide World Photos; pp. 4, 23, 29, 30, 31, 32, 36, 38,
39, 40, 42, 43, 44: AP/Wide World Photos.
Illustrations by Charles Shaw.